CHARITY AFIRE

Daughters of Charity
Civil War Nurses

Edited by
Betty Ann McNeil, D.C.

Virginia
1861–1865

D1279639

Civil War Trilogy

Other titles about the Civil War are available for purchase through the Gift Shop of the National Shrine of Saint Elizabeth Ann Seton:

The National Shrine of Saint Elizabeth Ann Seton
Gift Shop
333 South Seton Avenue, Emmitsburg, MD 21727-9298 USA
301-447-7122 ▪ www.setonshrine.org ▪ Email: giftshopmanager@setonshrine.org

Credits:
Consultation: Lori L. Stewart, Executive Director, Seton Heritage Center.
Cover Design and Layout: Stephanie Mummert, Graphic Designer
Research & Technical Assistance: Daughters of Charity Archives, Emmitsburg, Maryland: Bonnie Weatherly, Selin James, and Mary Anne Weatherly
Illustrations: Wayne R. Warnock

About the Cover:

The seal of the Company of the Daughters of Charity of Saint Vincent de Paul (center) joins historic photographs of Civil War nurses, Sister Euphemia Blenkinsop (left) and Sister Marie Louise Caulfield (right), against a background of manuscript accounts of their experiences appearing in the Civil War Trilogy, Charity Afire. The seal of the Daughters of Charity represents a heart encompassed by flames, with the figure of Jesus crucified. It is surrounded by the motto: The Charity of Jesus crucified urges us. The charity of Jesus Christ crucified, which animates and sets afire the heart of the Daughter of Charity, urges her to hasten to the relief of every type of human misery.

Images courtesy Daughters of Charity Archives, Emmitsburg, Maryland, and Northeast Province, Albany, New York.

INTRODUCTION

Elizabeth Bayley Seton (1774-1821) founded the Sisters of Charity of St. Joseph's near Emmitsburg, Maryland, July 31, 1809.[1] This was the first Roman Catholic sisterhood native to the United States for apostolic religious women. The foundress was a saintly widow from New York who converted to Catholicism and opened a school for girls, first in Baltimore, then near Emmitsburg in Frederick County, Maryland. She was fondly called *Mother Seton*. For her mission, Elizabeth envisioned seeking out and serving the needy, especially individuals and families living in poverty. Her vision of mission included teaching children who lacked educational opportunities and caring for sick and dying persons in need of nursing care.

The National Shrine of Saint Elizabeth Ann Seton located in Emmitsburg, Maryland, is also the site of an 1863 Union encampment. Its historic homes are open to the public, including the one in which Union officers conducted a war council to prepare for the battle of Gettysburg. See www.setonshrine.org.

The mission begun in seventeenth-century France by Saint Vincent de Paul (1581-1660) and Saint Louis de Marillac (1591-1660) was identical to that of Mother Seton who adopted their *Common Rules* for the Daughters of Charity and modified it for use in nineteenth-century America. About thirty years after her death, as a result of developments subsequent to the French Revolution, the sisters of the Emmitsburg community united with the Daughters of Charity of Saint Vincent de Paul based in Paris, France, in 1850.[2] Afterwards the community at Emmitsburg assumed the name Daughters of Charity. For consistency, Daughters of Charity is used throughout this work.

St. Joseph's Central House, headquarters for the province of the United States of the Daughters of Charity remained in Frederick County near Emmitsburg. Civil War armies moved about in the area. Early in 1862, "a detachment of troops encamped near enough to the Central House for the noise of the cannon" to be heard.[3]

The Daughters of Charity were experienced in healthcare in America. Elizabeth desired to provide "nurses for the sick and poor."[4] The foundress described to a friend that people in the Emmitsburg area were "All happy to [apply to] the Daughters of Charity who are night and day devoted to the sick and ignorant."[5] The earliest nursing experiences of the Sisters of Charity were in home health care in northern Frederick County and the infirmaries at both St. Joseph's Academy and Mount St. Mary's College & Seminary. In 1823, they assumed management of nursing services at the Baltimore Infirmary, which later became the University of Maryland Hospital. There the sisters cared for all classes of patients, including those in the marine ward. In 1828, Sisters from Emmitsburg opened the first Catholic hospital west of the Mississippi in St. Louis, Missouri.

By the dawn of the Civil War the Sisters and Daughters of Charity had a record of over fifty years of serving needy persons of all faiths in the United States. There had been foundations as far north as New York (1817) and Massachusetts (1832) and beyond the Mississippi as far west as California (1852). The distinctive seventeenth-century peasant dress (with its large white-winged bonnet or *cornette* and blue-grey dress) was a familiar symbol of charity and compassion to those who witnessed the pioneer efforts of the sisters in education, health care, and social services. Some of the milestones in the expansion of their ministries in the United States include:[6] establishment of the first free Catholic school (Emmitsburg, 1810); management of the first Catholic orphanage (Philadelphia, 1814); and founding and administration of the first Catholic psychiatric hospital (Baltimore, 1840).

The Daughters of Charity had responded previously to medical emergencies during national crises including the public health epidemics of Asiatic cholera (1832-1833 and 1850) at Baltimore, Philadelphia, Boston, and elsewhere on the eastern seaboard to outbreaks of yellow fever (1855) and typhoid (1862). By 1861, the Daughters of Charity already had more than thirty years experience in American health care: having served in three public hospitals and twelve Catholic hospitals.[7] In their institutions the Daughters of Charity were noted for developing and adhering to strict standards and quality controls.

The sisters first involvement in battlefield nursing and military service in the United States was during the Civil War (1861-1865) and its aftermath.[8] When additional sisters were required to care for the wounded throughout the country, despite limited personnel, Daughters of Charity superiors sent as many sisters as possible even to the point of closing educational institutions in order to make personnel available for the war effort.[9]

Catholic sisters were the only well established group in the United States which could transmit a heritage of knowledge, skills and management ability within an organized system of nursing at the outbreak of the Civil War. Twelve separate religious communities contributed the services of over six hundred sister nurses during the Civil War. Only four of these communities had previous hospital experience in the United States.

"The Daughters of Charity...[were] known everywhere, they...[were] everywhere respected."[10] About one-third of all the Daughters of Charity in the United States served at more than sixty sites in fifteen states during the Civil War and rendered nursing care and spiritual assistance to victims from both the United States Army and the Confederate Army.[11] Detailed records were not made at the time since local missions were authorized to respond spontaneously as new needs emerged and "Sisters often went out in large groups in response to emergency calls from various sections, and while in the service, they frequently changed from one camp to another."[12] Computerization has facilitated a more accurate count of those involved and now totals more than three hundred Daughters of Charity, approximately eighty more than originally reported in the late nineteenth century.

There are numerous extant accounts written by Daughters of Charity who served at various sites. Some kept primitive diaries, others summarized their experiences, but most wrote accounts retroactively in response to a request of the Vincentian priest, Rev. J. Francis Burlando, C.M., (1814-1873), who was director of the Daughters of Charity province of the United States.[13] Burlando requested the information so that he could submit a report to general superiors in Paris "of the facts and incidents in connection with the sisters' labors during the time of the last war."[14]

Sometime after the accounts were compiled and sent to Paris, the documents were collated and preserved as a book of manuscript accounts of their Civil War nursing.[15] Gaps were noted and efforts made to glean further details from the sisters involved in military hospitals, ambulance corps, transport ships, field hospitals, caring for prisoners of war, etc. Over the years additional accounts were written and oral histories recorded of other experiences of Daughters of Charity as nurses during the Civil War. The *Civil War-Trilogy Charity Afire. Angels of the Battlefield. Daughters of Charity Civil War Nurses* offers compelling insights of the sister nurses about casualty and compassion in three states: Maryland, Pennsylvania, and Virginia.

The sisters responded effusively in many cases to Burlando's request for information about religious conversions and "anything interesting and edifying." These accounts reflect the spirituality of nineteenth-century America which formed the sisters in their piety, devotionalism, and religious zeal expressed through their charitable mission of mercy.

These personal accounts reflect the style, terms, and linguistics of the period, as well as the educational level and proficiency in writing and grammar of the sisters whose vocabulary mirrors the social and cultural realities of nineteenth-century America. During the war years the sisters were most concerned about accomplishing their mission and being effective in their ministry and not about bequeathing details for the historical record. Their legacy is best exemplified in their heroic lives of self-sacrificial dedication and non-discriminatory service to the sick and wounded of both the North and the South. Their dedication to render quality nursing care to all casualties contributed greatly to diminishing religious prejudice, particularly toward Roman Catholics. At Gettysburg one eyewitness to a touching deathbed scene said with great emotion to his fellow soldiers: "I have often heard of Daughters of Charity, and I can now testify to their having the right name."

Other branches of the Sisters of Charity were involved in Civil War nursing, most notably the Sisters of Charity of Cincinnati and the Sisters of Charity of New York. There are additional communities of apostolic women who trace their roots to the foundation at Emmitsburg, including the Sisters of Charity of Saint Elizabeth (New Jersey), the Sisters of Charity of Seton Hill (Pennsylvania), and the Sisters of Charity of Halifax (Nova Scotia). Today these communities, along with others and the Daughters of Charity of the North American provinces, collaborate through the Sisters of Charity Federation. In this way the torch of the Seton legacy continues to be passed to future generations who stand on the shoulders of the courageous women of the Civil War era. Their compassionate care to the sick and wounded on the battlefield, in ambulances, and hospital transports gave dramatic witness to their convictions of faith as they quietly and humbly carried out their *mission of charity* as Civil War nurses—angels of the battlefield.

Sister Loyola Law, D.C., (1834-1906), extracted, consolidated, and edited, the manuscript of these personal accounts and produced into three volumes of *Annals of the Civil War* at the dawn of the twentieth century.[16] Extracts from different accounts by eye witnesses in the same circumstances resulted in the inclusion of some duplicate material. Nevertheless, Sister Loyola's typescripts, which are organized by site or locale of service, have been consulted by researchers over the last century. Despite minor editorial changes for stylistics, spelling, and format, *Charity Afire. Virginia—1861-1865,* the first of the *Civil War Trilogy* preserves the content of the *Annals of the Civil War* (Law, 1904) but also includes annotations and reorganizes the sequence for clarity. Selected information has been added in brackets for identification of individuals, e.g. "sister servant [local superior]" and ease of comprehension.

For the convenience of students of the Civil War an annotated version of the 1904 edition of *Annals of the Civil War* entitled *The Daughters of Charity in the Civil War* (B.A. McNeil, 2002) is on deposit in research libraries at the following locations: Chimborazo Medical Museum, Richmond National Battlefield Park, Richmond, Virginia; Gettysburg National Military Park, Gettysburg, Pennsylvania; and the National Museum of Civil War Medicine, Frederick, Maryland.

Sister Matilda Coskery was one of the Daughters of Charity who distinguished herself as a nurse during the war years. Her accounts document the compassionate competence of the sisters at Harpers Ferry and Winchester, Virginia; Antietam, Boonsboro, and Frederick, Maryland, and Gettysburg, Pennsylvania. She was an oracle in the field of nursing in the mid-nineteenth century. Sister Matilda is featured in a historical study of the Daughters of Charity contributions to nursing in the United States in *Enlightened Charity: The Holistic Nursing Care, Education, and Advices Concerning the Sick of Sister Matilda Coskery (1799–1870)*, Martha Libster PhD, RN, CNS and Sister Betty Ann McNeil, D.C., (Golden Apple Publications, 2009).

The subjects of the Civil War Trilogy-Charity Afire include Virginia, Maryland, and Pennsylvania. Other works about the Daughters of Charity role during the Civil War are being prepared for publication in the near future. An annotated edition of the Annals of the Civil War (1904) is forthcoming as Dear Masters-Daughters of Charity Civil War Nurses. An unabridged and fully annotated compilation of the Daughters of Charity Civil War records, is being prepared for publication. Balm of Hope will make source documents and valuable historical records available to the public.

Betty Ann McNeil, D.C., Archivist
Daughters of Charity
Emmitsburg, Maryland
4 January 2011

RICHMOND

The *Infirmary of St. Francis de Sales* had been in operation by the sisters for the Sick in general, when the war having commenced, this house was soon made use of for the sick soldiers. The first appeal in Virginia was made May 16, 1861, to the sisters by the [Confederate] Medical Authorities, to admit their men for treatment. But very soon this building was too crowded for their benefit.[17] The Government then took a very large house, or houses, making this a hospital. They thought their male nurses would serve their purpose, but, in a few days the Surgeon and Officers in charge, came to the sisters of the [St. Francis de Sales] Infirmary and [St. Joseph's] Asylum, begging them to come to their assistance, as the poor men were much in need of them.

We went to *St. Ann's Military Hospital* June 26th of the same year.[18] All kinds of misery lay outstretched before us. It was 10:00 a.m. but not one of these several hundred had had any nourishment up to this hour. Our first lesson received, was of patience for, in this field of suffering, scarcely a moan was heard, except that attendant on the last struggle of death. The sufferer's poor two fold nature, or existence, claimed assistance in an imperative voice. Our poor sisters seemed only as means of a tender, merciful Providence, moving and suggesting to each one what to do, or what to postpone. As for reflection, or consideration, there was none. God directed, and He needed not to deliberate.

New arrivals of wounded men [from Manassas] added much to our distress, as no more beds were unoccupied, so they were lain on the floor, and the poor sisters were happy to place even a bundle of shavings, or old paper under their wounded heads for pillows. Weary as the sisters were, they could not sleep, when indeed they were able to leave the dying men, for the heavy smell of death that seemed to fill their lodgings. They at last looked for the cause of this horrid stench, and found in an adjoining room amputated limbs of a week's standing, falling even into corruption.

Sometimes the good sister servants [local superiors] of *St. Joseph's Orphan Asylum* and the *Infirmary of St. Francis de Sales*, would send by turns sisters to aid us a little. Upon one of these occasions, a man speechless and dying, gave strong evidences of desiring baptism and received it.[19] The next day another sister waited on that Ward, and finding this dying man, the same efforts to aid his poor soul were made by our zealous sister; the conclusion was, the good priest was called and the dying man was again baptized after which he died. We could only console ourselves in the hope, that the Providence of our dear Lord directed the matter.

Baptisms and conversions were numerous, and it was glorious to hear the dying men invoking our Blessed Mother [Virgin Mary] so devotedly, though for the first and last time in their lives. Late one night, a Protestant doctor called us and asked if we could not do something for a wretched man, who was dying awfully. He was in great anguish mentally and bodily. We spoke of baptism to him, but to this he would say, "What do I know of it?" He seemed to be possessed by an evil spirit. A sister gave him blessed water in his drink...presently one took the relic of Saint Vincent, put it under his head, and in a few seconds a decided consent for baptism was obtained and accordingly given. He became composed, and the sisters continued making [prayerful] aspirations, hardly knowing whether he heard or understood, when presently they heard him invoking Jesus and Mary. We left him, but in the morning the nurse told us he had continued to call on the holy name of Jesus to the very last.

A poor negligent Catholic was so touched by the admonition of a sister, that he really began his confession to her. She stopped him, and the priest was soon with him and prepared him for death. A lad was spoken to of baptism, some little instruction followed on the Blessed Trinity, the Incarnation, the Sacrament of Baptism, etc., when he suddenly cried out: "O, sister, baptize me, baptize me in the name of the Father, and of the Son and of the Holy Ghost." He occupied himself in prayer after his baptism, saying often: "My God, this is a deathbed repentance, but, "Oh! Have mercy on my poor soul."

During August, the same year, several sisters from St. Joseph's [Emmitsburg] came to our relief, but as hostilities progressed, so also did our duties multiply. A nurse meeting with contradictions one day, cried out impatiently: "I am neither an Angel nor a Sister of Charity, and will not put up with this thing."

One poor soldier seemed determined to die as he had lived, but at last told the nurse to call a minister to him. He came, looked at him, and finding him sinking, said: "Nothing can be done for this man. He is dying." Then he walked away. Opposite to this poor fellow, the priest was preparing a dying man for death. The other gaining a little strength, called the sister and said to her, "I heard my minister say he could do nothing for me, while my companion there has every hope in the spiritual helps he has received. Therefore, if my church can do nothing for me when I am dying, I renounce it." He was soon prepared by our holy religion for his happy exit [from this life].

Other hospitals in or around Richmond were commenced and the Government demanded sisters; but all, this side of the Blockade were in Military Posts, except those engaged with our orphans, the day schools having been closed for the time. As our sisters were to be sent to these different hospitals, the number for each was small. Some continued only for some months, circumstances calling for change of place, etc. In preparing for one of these temporary labors, the head sister said: "Oh! Let us not forget our little bell.[20] For we cannot do much good unless we get our spiritual exercises," but, Alas! We were there several days before the bell was heard to sound. Mass, meditations, chaplet, reading, etc., were included in our heartfelt efforts to gain heaven for the poor wandering, but redeemed souls of Jesus Christ.

We can say that, in each and every location of the kind, there were many baptisms for the dying, conversions among the convalescent, and sincere returns of the careless Catholic. A sister would say to another; "Do you know how many have been baptized or converted?" "No, truly," was the reply: "I began to keep account, but I feared our dear Lord would be displeased, and I discontinued it." Upon our arrival at one of these hospitals, a man lay dead whose interment was about taking place. Sister said to the steward: "This man must have died in terrible agony." "Yes," said he, "he died blaspheming God, and cursing everyone around him." But thanks to our sweet Jesus, we witnessed no such horrible scenes...not another death like this occurred here.

One of our stewards was very gentlemanly in his manners, and a scholar of about forty years of age. He called himself, "Like to St. Paul, as to zeal, in his hatred of Catholicity." He said to a sister: "I admire you Ladies for your great charity, but I despise your religion." Sister calmly replied: "Without our Holy Religion, sir, we would have no Charity." He left the Army sometime after, and on his arrival, his brother gave a dinner and invited friends. The conversation fell upon Catholic errors, absurdities, etc., of which, formerly, our steward had been the warmest in his bitterness, but to their surprise, he suddenly interrupted them, saying: "Gentlemen, in my presence I will allow nothing said against the Catholics. I once thought I gave glory to God by opposing that religion but, I am changed on this matter. You may think me crazy, but I watched those Daughters of Charity day and night, waiting on our sick and wounded men; and never did a frown darken their features, and I now feel convinced, that the Catholic Religion alone can give such proofs of heroic virtue as I have witnessed in those sisters, and I intend to embrace their religion."

Soon after going to one of these new hospitals, the Surgeon in charge said to us: I am obliged to make known our difficulties to you that you may enable me to surmount them, for you Ladies accomplish all you undertake. Until now we have been supplied in the delicacies necessary for our patients from Louisiana, but the Blockade now prevents this, and I fear to enter the wards, as the poor men are still asking for former refreshments, and they cannot be quieted. We dislike also letting them know the straits we are in, though this hindrance may be of short duration." The poor sisters hardly saw how to aid matters, but proposed that wagons might be sent among the farm houses, and gather fowl, milk, butter, fruit, etc., etc. This was done, but in the meantime complaints had been made to headquarters, "that since the sisters had come to the hospital, all delicacies had been withheld from the poor sick." The surgeon and sisters knew nothing of this until a deputy arrived to learn the truth of the charge. They visited the wards during meals, after which they entered the room where the sisters dined. They then told the surgeon the motive of their visit. He was glad to explain to them the cause of the complaints. The deputy informed the Soldiers that the good sisters were not the cause of their suffering, that their fare was always worse still, than they gave to them, for when there is not enough of what is good, they take what is worse for themselves.

A terrible engagement commencing near the City, (Richmond) this hospital being more convenient was made the field hospital [Howard's Grove], where all the wounded were first brought, their wounds examined and dressed, then sent to other hospitals to make room for others. This Battle lasted 7 days, commencing about 2:00 a.m. and continuing to 10 p.m. each day.[21] The bombs were bursting and reddening the heavens while the Reserve Corps ranged about three hundred yards from our door. While these days lasted, our poor sisters in the City Hospitals were shaken by the cannonading and the heavy rolling of the ambulances filling the streets bringing in the wounded and dying men. The entire city trembled as if from earthquakes during the whole week, with one exception of the few short hours between 10 and 2:00 o'clock. Memory is surfeited over these days, hearts overflowing with anguish at the bare remembrance of them, but, to lay the scene truly before you is beyond any human pen.

The soldiers told us that they had received orders from their generals to capture Daughters of Charity if they could, as the hospitals were in such great need of them. One night the doctors called us to go and see a man whose limb must be amputated, but he would not consent to take the lulling dose without hearing the Daughters of Charity say he could do so. The sisters said, it was dark and the crowd was too great to think of going. They left, but soon returned declaring the man's life depended on their coming, since he would not otherwise comply. Two sisters then, escorted by the good doctors went to him, who seeing them said, "Sisters, they wish me to take a dose that will deprive me of my senses. I wish to make my confession first, and the priest is not here." Sister told him that he might safely take it and she would try and find the priest for him. She then sent for the good priest, who soon was able to put the poor man at peace. We continued our visits to him during his days of martyrdom, and we never saw evidences of greater virtue. We thanked our dear Lord for allowing us such an example of Christian patience. Another man was dying, the nurse called us up to go to him. Several doctors were around his bed. Sister spoke to him of Baptism. He earnestly desired it, and after a preparation for it, sister baptized him. One of the doctors said: "Sister, do you think that will do him any good?" Sister answered him very calmly: "I think nothing. I know it will help him."

We could rarely ask them if they wished to become Catholics, for so many early objections were then recalled to their minds that they felt deterred. But simply, when death seemed near, and after the essentials were gained, we asked them "if they did not wish to become Children of God in the Religion established by our Divine Savior." Though many also said: "Sisters, although I have heard many terrible things against your Church, yet the Religion that teaches what I see you do, must indeed be a true one, and I wish to belong to it." These remarks were of very frequent occurrence.

[Sometimes the poor men were brought to us from encampments of great scarcity, or from hospitals, from which the able-bodied had suddenly retreated, and left perhaps thousands of wounded, and prisoners, who in their distress had fed on mule flesh, rats, even the entrails of cattle,] after the meat had failed to be sufficient.[22] These poor creatures on arriving among us looked like dead men, and almost without desires, at least, without voice sufficient to express them. For many such, it seemed as if the Angel Guardian of each had kept life flowing until the Saving Waters of, or words of Salvation had been applied [John 3:5].

Our hospitals were often also extremely scarce of the necessities of life, but, we thanked our dear Lord that our sisters seemed not to feel their own privations if they could obtain something for the sick, wounded and starving "Members of our Jesus." For our own table, rough corn bread and strong fat bacon were luxuries, provided the dear sufferers were better served. As for beverage, we could not always tell what they gave us for coffee or tea; for, at one time it would be sage, or some other herb, roots, beans, etc., etc. But through all we seemed to be refreshed or supported by that invisible Bread—The Divine Will. Some constitutions among the sisters were most weak and delicate.

As the War continued, the Government made use of the *Infirmary of St. Francis de Sales,* the Sisters' Hospital, also, for their soldiers. Here all things were directed by the sisters, and the Government paid them so much. Here, too, our sisters could do much more for their patients. During the time their house was thus occupied, about 2,500 patients (soldiers) were admitted, of whom but one hundred died. Many, many were brought to know their duty to God and their own souls. The Blessed Sacrament was kept in our little Chapel, and often a sick Chaplain would share our hospitality and thus we had Mass more frequently, and the sick likewise, more instruction. No negligent Catholics rejected the kind persuasions of the sisters, who urged them to a return of their Christian obligations. Even the friends, who visited them, were induced to observe their religious duties. We had also the great satisfaction of seeing our poor men enter earnestly into the Spirit of the Church, by returns of her various Festivals, in this, our own Hospital.

St. Ann's Military Hospital continued to be thus occupied until the close of the War. Every day brought some new incident before us, but, the poor daughters of Saint Vincent trusted only to the graces of their holy vocation to meet and discharge them properly.

Upon one occasion lady prisoners were brought to us for safe keeping, who otherwise must have been consigned to a common jail. Another time a female soldier is brought to us that she might be taught to know her place and character in life. The apprenticeship of this poor girl had been novel reading. One leap more, and she stands in soldiers' ranks, flushed with the thoughts of the laurels that await her. However, Saint Vincent sees her afar off. He instructs her on better things and she is soon the "humble Christian," ashamed, and tutored for Heaven by the edification she continues to give.

And O, how many were taught to know the love and honor due to the Holy Mother of our Redeemer! All desired to have her [Miraculous] Medal. The sisters told the Soldiers, that we loved her as they loved their flag, and that if we honored her, She would protect us, as they hoped for all good from their flag. One, after his return to a far distant State, wrote to the sisters for a Medal, saying he had lost his.

Evacuation of Richmond. We may, perhaps, make some remarks on our conditions at the time the City [of Richmond] was evacuated, and the surrendering of the [Confederate] Army took place.

Notwithstanding the foresight of the authorities on the defeat, still, its arrival was of most appalling excitement. Medical stores, commissary departments and houses of merchandise were thrown open. Liquors flowed down the streets, that preventing its dangerous effects, some confusion might be spared. Stores became public property. Our poor City was trembling from the blowing up of the gunboats in the river that bounded the City on the east.

A youth was very low and not baptized; sister said, "Did you never read in the Bible that you must be baptized before you could enter Heaven?" He answered: "I cannot read." Then sister gave him some instructions. Some hours after a minister talked and prayed by him, but said nothing of baptism. Later sister asked him if he desired baptism? He did, and received it. The minister coming again to see him, the poor boy only said to him, "I do not wish you to visit me." This surprised us, for we had said nothing of the sort to him. He died soon after.

A dying man, a Protestant, was requested to make his peace with God, one evening, but he begged to postpone it for the morning. Sister said: "You are very low." "Yes," he said: "But I cannot speak strong enough now, let me wait until tomorrow." Oh! said sister, will you live till then? "If you say a prayer to ask that I may, I <u>will</u>," he replied. She could not insist for fear his forced compliance might be injurious to him, so all she could do was truly to pray, as he had told her. In the morning he was able and very calmly expired.

One poor man positively refused all observations concerning his soul's welfare. Sister secreted a medal under his pillow. He soon became restless and bade the nurses remove that pillow and give him another. The nurse being a good Catholic told sister. She told him to drop the medal in the case of the other! Soon, this pillow was objected to and he would have none. Then the Medal was fastened to the mattress. In a very short time he declared, he could not rest on the bed either, and would lie on floor. He died there, in a little time after, as he had lived.

A Protestant minister passing around said to a young soldier: "What is your religion, my Son?" "I have none," was the reply. "What were your parents?" "They were Baptists. Ah! That is the true Religion," he said. "These Catholics sprang from the Baptists." He then goes to the next bed, saying to another youth: "What is your religion?" "I have none," he said, "and my parents also were without any." "Well, my Son," said the good minister, "you must pray hard and hold fast to your religion, or you will lose your faith." "How can I lose what I have not got?" said the boy. But he passed on to a third one. Beginning his questions here also, the boy said with quickness: "I do not wish you to speak to me of religion," "Will you have a drink, my son, or what can I do for you?" "Call sister to me," he answered. Sister came, and the poor boy burst into tears saying: "Sister send him away, I do not care for his Religion. I am a Catholic." The poor minister bowed and left them. Sister then said, "you have not told me you were a Catholic." "When I was a child," he said, "I was very sickly. My parents lived in the wild woods, and no minister lived near us. A traveling priest called one dark night at our door and asked for lodging or shelter. They expected me to die that night, and my mother finding he was a minister of the Gospel, asked him to baptize me. He did so, and the next day I was well. My mother, therefore, always told me, the good Gentleman had baptized me a Catholic, and that was all I knew of the Catholics till I came here. But, now sister, I have resolved to live as a Catholic, so please give me a book that will tell me what I have to do." The Catechism soon became his hourly occupation; truth was making such active progress on his young heart. He soon made his confession and was preparing for Communion, when he was removed to the Convalescent Corps. But we have cause to hope for his perseverance.

These, though many, are still but few of the numberless conversions, baptisms at death, and returns of the careless Catholics, which our sisters witnessed in and around Richmond, in the various hospitals where they were occupied. Memory cannot retain detailed instances, but it can vouch to the pleasing fact that refusals to the spiritual assistance offered to them, were exceedingly rare, scarcely one to fifty during those days of slaughter and death.

Towards morning we thought it better to secure the Holy Mass early, for fear of what a few hours more might show forth. We were preparing for it, when suddenly a terrific explosion stunned, as it were, the power of thought. The noise of the breaking of windows in our Hospital and neighboring dwellings added greatly to the alarm, as it seemed for the moment, as an entire destruction. Fearing it might be the bursting of the first shells, the good Chaplain thought it better to give the Holy Communion to the sisters, and then consume the blessed hosts. Presently, however, we learned that the Confederates had blown up their own supplies of powder, which were very near us. Then followed the explosion of all the Government buildings. We passed that eventful day with as much composure as our trust in our good Lord enabled us to do, though, from time to time, we were in evident danger of having our House, with its helpless inmates, all destroyed.

After the surrender, a Federal Officer rode up to the door, told us we were perfectly safe, that property should be respected, that he would send a guard to protect the house, etc. His visit was fortunate, for, presently a band of Negroes came and ordered our doors to be opened.. The sisters pretending not to understand them were slow to obey, and this caused one to say out very imperatively: "Open dem gates, whose property dis?" "Oh," said sister, "this belongs to the Sisters of Charity. Col. D. ...has been here, everything has been attended to, all is right." He immediately passed the words to his comrades, and they rode off.

Our sisters from the various hospitals took homeward directions, with hearts and minds still more weary than their bodies.

The approach of the Federals placed our hospital [in Lynchburg] in imminent danger and it was decided to move the sick and the hospital stores to Richmond [in February 1865]. The Surgeon General [Samuel Moore] of the Confederate Army begged that we would take charge of the *Stuart Hospital* in that city [Richmond], which we did on the 13th of February 1865. Father Gache accompanied us and continued his mission of zeal and charity.

We were ten in number and as usual, we found plenty to do, to place the sick in a comfortable situation, which we had just accomplished when the city [Richmond] was evacuated, and on the 13th of April, the Hospital being dispensed with, we left Richmond for our "sweet valley home" [at Emmitsburg].

St. Francis de Sales Infirmary of Richmond having completed the number that the Institution can comfortably accommodate, and the sisters of the said Institution, being sufficient to supply the wants of the inmates, the latter part of July found our sisters of the [St. Joseph's] Asylum with nothing but good desires whereon to feed their zeal. We knew that the soldiers had been removed to the General Hospital where they suffered for want of proper care but <u>we</u> were tied down [here with obligations at the Infirmary].[23] We could not volunteer our services and the Rt. Rev. Bishop [John McGill] seemed entirely opposed to any hospital or infirmary which might prove an obstacle to the prosperity of that of St. Francis de Sales.[24]

Matters so stood when a letter was received from our kind Mother [Ann Simeon Norris] regretting that we could not aid in the noble work; still, no formal application had been made for our services, but on the morrow of the reception of Mother's letter, Doctor [Charles Bell] Gibson called soliciting sisters most earnestly to come to the relief of the sufferers who really were such. But, how to soften the good Bishop's heart! Prayers were said to the Blessed Mother and the Saints to render him propitious; and with a feeling described as akin to that of Judith when she went to "amputate" Holofernes' head, did we go to the Episcopal Palace to cut the knot that held us from our work.[25] At last consent was obtained, and joyfully was it announced that on the following Saturday possession would be given us. Immediately hands were busy in fashioning working aprons, and in collecting the few indispensable articles required for our migration. At last we started; twenty minutes walk brought us before a noble looking structure of brick originally intended for an Alms House.[26] It is in an unfinished state; the walls unplastered mostly, but thoroughly ventilated and free from dampness.

St. Ann's Military Hospital—Richmond General Hospital

After some hours of tedious waiting, we were introduced to our duty. Imagine wards filled with about twelve or fourteen men, the rooms opening one into another, the house containing about three hundred patients who at that late hour advancing onto 12 o'clock had not yet broken their fast. On all sides we encountered unemptied pans and in our dismay found out it was the habit of the nurse to discharge such vessels "sans ceremonie" over the porch into the yard below.

The sight of the wounded and sick was distressing, and our first care was to provide some things to relieve their hunger. To effect this, we went to the kitchen making the acquaintance of Nicholas the cook, black George, and other occupants of this section of the house, who though good men and doing their best, succeeded but poorly in having an orderly kitchen. Adjoining the kitchen is the store room. Then it contained not one cupboard, but three long tables upon which were placed "petit mele", the delicacies sent by the ladies, and the bread furnished by the house. Breakfast was over—after that we looked about to see how we could manage to get things in some sort of order. One sister being detained at home later than the others and arriving at the hospital, burning with zeal to be of use to everybody, suddenly found her career of usefulness checked by another sister who possessed by the spirits of order locked up the pantry not perceiving she was in it. Another of our sisters was deprived of her nurse, who from the wards was obliged to be transferred to the "lock-up." Notwithstanding all the inconveniences, faces brightened at the fact that the sisters were going to take care of them. Faces of all save of the washer woman who, from a mistaken sense of duty, we suppose, <u>watched</u> instead of washed a pile of dirty sheets. Some ladies, too, were disposed to much talk, but generally they were quiet and kindly consigned to our care, the delicacies they had brought for distribution. Really, we enjoyed that day, and if fault was committed, it was that we were too generous in feeding the hungry soldiers, some of whom declared they had not had such a meal for a long time. Night came on and with it the reluctant close of our labors. Four of our sisters were to remain at the hospital at night by turns. We who were to go home bade them goodnight and found at the door the ambulance or carriage used for the transportation of the sick and wounded soldiers, awaiting our command.[27] In we got and rode home with the expression of St. Francis Xavier in our hearts and on our lips "too much, O Lord, too much!"

Our sisters that night got no sleep, for the wants of the sufferers were passing and the pillow was joyfully relinquished for the vigil. The next morning was Sunday. After Mass we went to the relief of our sisters. The way we now give the meals is this: each ward has its messroom. The food is brought there, measured out, and sent into the wards by the nurses. The second day was passed as the first, but for Sister Blanche DeLaney [sic, Rooney] there was a multiplication of the loaves for the supply, though slim, was found sufficient.[28] We have in this hospital our brave Southern men and the wounded men of the North, and oh! How they suffer! Some of them, whose legs were amputated, were swarming with maggots. After the dressing of one man's leg, I remember actually sweeping these maggots away. Yet so patient are the poor creatures, you seldom hear a complaint and they are most grateful for every little act of kindness. The poor fellow whose leg had been cut off called sister to his bedside and in a low voice, said: "You know the doctor thinks I may not live over night, therefore, I have a great favor to ask that I hope you won't refuse--I have a mother," (tears checked his utterance) and the sister said, "I understand, you want me to write to her?" "Yes, tell her that her child is dead but don't tell her how I have suffered; that would break her heart." Towards night about fifty wounded soldiers—prisoners from Manassas—were brought in at once; some dying, others wounded, and until better accommodations could be provided they had to be laid on the floor where they lay, some scarcely covered. Sister called out, "Do, sister, get me something for this poor fellow's head, he has just asked me for a log of wood." The sister went out, but where to get a pillow since everyone was engaged. At last a pillow case was found and the bright idea came to the sister, "I'll stuff it with paper." She brought it to the Yankee thinking the invention suited the individual for whom it was destined. The poor fellow smiled as it was given to him. Then sister said, "Take this blanket over to that man." Poor fellow! Nothing covered his shoulders but his scapulars. Another came in so dreadfully wounded in the cheek that the sister actually mistook the wound for his mouth and was presenting his nourishment there. Another came in, shot through the shin. A few words convinced us he was a Catholic. He was in danger; therefore, we made him make the acts of contrition and resignation, and prepared him for death. The priest came that night and I believe the poor fellow was anointed and died.

At last we left for bed, but when we got quietly fixed in our room, Sister Blanche [Rooney] said, "I can't sleep; there is such a smell of death." The morrow unraveled the secret for in the next room were found a pair of legs amputated the week before. Sister says it was a big trial to visit that room— she stuffed her nose and mouth with her handkerchief and threw open the window, the stench was horrible indeed. Now this inconvenience is removed, the limbs interred at once. The other day one man was buried with three legs!!!

On Sunday we also received an addition to our number of wounded in the person of some of the Federal officers—their number soon amounted to eleven and now the garret to which they were elevated accommodates many more. When I say garret, I mean you to understand that they are fine, airy rooms, as are all the apartments of the General Hospital and these rooms being the most private in the house, and the most suitable for them. The accompanying drawing will give some idea of our wards.[29] On the Officers' quarters were found Captains, Majors, Lieutenants, Sergeants, etc.; poor fellows all wounded; not many of them very seriously however. One fellow blessed with a fine voice had a guitar loaned him and you may see him in the corner "whiling away the dull hours." In this ward Sister Aimee [Butterley] is stationed and it seems the employment suits her, for by the sketch she has grown very much since her arrival in Richmond. Sometimes these poor officers are rather importuned by visitors who are untiring in their questions. "Whar's you wounded? Whar's you shot at?" (meaning, what part of the body). "Shot at Manassas" was the laconic reply.

As one of our sisters was crossing the porch, a tall brawny soldier cried out, "you ladies have a sight of work to do, but I tell you that you get high pay." "None at all" was the answer. "What" said he, starting back with surprise, "You don't tell me you do all this work for nothing?" One of the nurses or hands about the place, being sadly put out about something that went wrong, explained that he was neither an angel nor a Sister of Charity, and he would not put up with it at all. I propose now, giving some attached sketches [descriptions] both of the spiritual and physical order, hoping they will contribute to your edification and amusement.

Double Baptism. On one occasion, the sister of wards T and U, being called off, her place was supplied by another who seeing a poor man whose leg had been amputated and who besides, shot through the lungs, was in a horrible condition, apparently with but few hours of life before him. Her zeal was enkindled and kneeling beside him as he lay upon a mattress on the floor; she endeavored to learn if he had been baptized or if he desired baptism. A few trembling words that she could scarcely make out; a required signal of the hand, at last assured her there was good disposition and sufficient evidence of desire for the sacrament. Accordingly when the priest came, it was administered conditionally. The medal of Our Lady was placed under the man's head, and all day long the sister improved her little opportunities of preparing his poor soul. In the evening she found out on her return home to state the joyous news of her success. "What!" exclaimed the sister of the ward after ascertaining the locality of the patient, "Sister, I baptized that man last night, thus with two baptisms and two medals, he made his way, I hope, to a blessed eternity."

Conversions. We have had some most consoling conversions—one, a young man who was baptized and anointed, dying two days after his sentiments were so beautiful as the good Father spoke to him of contrition for his sins. He could not restrain his sighs and tears. It's so comforting to hear them call on our Blessed Mother, as it were for the first and last time. One night it was late but one of the doctors had come to us to ask if we could do nothing for the soul of a poor man who was dying. The poor wretch lay groaning and gasping, and to questions relative to baptism he could cry out, "What do I know about it?" He put us in mind of a possessed person. It seemed a hopeless case. Again the sisters went to his bedside, this time one of us adopted the plan of giving him holy water to drink, still though some ray of hope appeared we again left him in a most sad state.[14] The third time one of the sisters picked up a relic of St. Vincent with the feeling that the case was a desperate one and our Holy Father must assist her; she put it under the head of the dying man. A few seconds after a decided consent was obtained for baptism which was given. The poor boy became calm though suffering much. We continued to make aspirations [brief prayers] for him, scarcely knowing if he understood them, when we were presently rewarded by hearing him invoke the name of Jesus. These two cases were among our Southern men.

In the Northern ward, a man was in danger of dying. Sister thought he was a Catholic and on inquiry found her suspicion confirmed, but like many others the man had neglected the one thing necessary. A few words from sister brought him to a sense of his duty, and so penetrated was he with the sense of his situation, and sorrow for having been such a bad boy, that he actually commenced his confession to sister who stopped him, bidding him to await the priest who came afterwards, heard his confession and anointed him. I do not remember if he received Holy Communion, but the Fathers do bring the Blessed Sacrament with them and several have had the happiness of being strengthened by that heavenly food. In one of the wards you will find a colored boy. He was taken at Manassas, having been the servant of one of the Federal captains. He was shot near the lungs, the ball penetrating the back and breast. The poor boy is looked upon as a curiosity for the report got about that he was a preacher which, however, is false. Since he entered the hospital, he asked for baptism—it has been given him, also Extreme Unction. He is most assiduous in the study of his catechism, and as his health seems to be improving we already think he would prove an excellent help should he entirely recover.

The Minister's Visit. One of Sister Philip's patients, having it appear, made it a rule with himself not to let the day go by without asking for something, would constantly call her to his bedside with, "Please, sister, give me a sheet," or, "Please sister, get me some rice." "Please this" and "Please that"—well one day he said, "Sister please get me a Methodist minister." Sister said for her part she knew no minister but if he would ask the doctor, one could be brought. The request was made and in came the minister who remained sometime with the patient. On going to him after the visit, sister made some remark that she supposed he was glad he had seen the minister. "O, Yes!" said he, clasping his hands. "O, yes, he promised me a soft bed."

Fearing that you may think we are too much sated with our success, I beg our sisters to recall an expression of Sister Mary Ann ("that the sisters first get a puff [affirmation] and then get a buff [rebuff]!")

There is one of our Southern soldiers ill, who certainly cannot live, but some ten days or so. One morning, seeing him so sick and weak, sister asked him if he had been baptized. "No," was the answer (the man's mind was perfectly sound). "No, I am a musician that is all I know!" The sister said that music was a delightful thing, that she had even taught it herself, but now could teach him something far better whereupon the man shook his head, for he could take a fiddle and on one string could play anything. Besides he urged that he had never harmed anyone and he believed that what he was now punished for, was for joining that regiment when he knew his constitution was illy [poorly] calculated for it. Still the sister represented the impossibility of a salvation without the sacrament and seeing the moment for conviction was unfavorable, she said, "Now you must try to think of this." The man looked at her and said, "In one ear and out of the other." It makes an impression! Nevertheless, we must not give him up, and we may yet get our poor musician at the last hour.

The Emetic. An emetic having been ordered to one of the patients who was very ill and quite out of his head, the sister administered it and had in good preparation the basin and pitcher of hot water, but lo! The emetic had no effect. She went to the doctor and related the case. "Give another" was the answer! It was given; still the emetic had no effect. Some time passed, again the sister went to the doctor who presented a pint of hot water (down the man's throat who was out of his head). The sister went by the bedside and in spite of himself the man was obedient and drank a part. The doctors came in and stood by the bed. Again the sister stated there had been no effect. She noticed a strange expression on the doctors' countenance and one of them quietly walked away. The sister thought him rather indifferent, but it was not until one of them turning aside, asked for a clean shirt for the poor man, she realized the fact that an emetic can have two effects.

The Garret. We lost some of the prisoners from the Officers' quarters. They were so far recovered that they could be removed from the hospital to another large building called the tobacco factory. They were lavish in their expressions of gratitude towards the sisters for the kind attention they had received—almost all left with the little medal and with a promise ever to keep it. They left with guards below and behind as is always the case in such circumstances. Five of of them clubbed together and sent sister a check of Fifty Dollars for the orphans [at St. Joseph's Asylum]. Among the number still left at the hospital there is a lady most respectably connected, a family friend of the Setons, and of Major Harper.[31] Hearing her husband had been killed at Manassas, she came on hoping to get his body, when to her joy she found him only wounded. Determined to share his fate she accompanied him to Richmond. Whilst on the way, some of the prisoners asked the conductor, "Where are you going to take us?" "To the Poor House," was the reply. "Do you hear that, my dear," said the affrighted lady, "They are going to take us to the poor house." Glad enough was she afterwards to find it was a poor house only in name. Her devotion to her husband is beautiful. She is there only for him and troubles herself about nothing else, and seems to be a lovely modest woman. Her husband is Captain Rickets of the Federal Army.[32] Notwithstanding good will, nature sometimes experiences not a little fatigue and it would seem a most tempting time to repair this loss is during meditation. One of our sisters remarked the other day that she felt very mean, indeed, to "thank God for the graces we have received during our meditation," when she was conscious of having slept all the time.

We were all much rejoiced at the edifying sentiments of a young man who it appears was dying, when sister went to him and found that he had never been baptized. I believe she asked him if he desired baptism. "Yes," was the reply. Then a few words of instruction were given of baptism, the Incarnation of the Second Person of the Blessed Trinity, etc. "Oh! Baptize me" said the poor boy. "Baptize me in the name of the Father and of the Son and of the Holy Ghost." sister told him he should have his desire. A priest came in and thought that if the patient lived it would be better to defer the sacrament in order to secure further instruction, but he told sister that should there be danger, to baptize him, herself. In the night she was obliged to do it. The sentiments of the poor man were beautiful. "It is true, my God," he cried out, "This is a deathbed repentance, but oh! have mercy on my poor soul."

It is most consoling to see the ease with which those men are induced to go to confession. Sometimes the priest will sit on the porch with his penitent at his side, the other boys who are preparing, walk up and down the porch as if they were taking exercises.

Having no chapel at the ho use, one certainly must be in earnest to go to confession under much inconvenience. In giving Holy Communion the good Father made use of his hat for a little altar upon which he put our Lord, for it was a cleaner place than a hospital table.

The Kitchen. Oh that I could sketch this region of the house! All good housekeepers would be in wonderment. In the first place, without exaggeration, the stove might be twice as large as it is and no harm to it. Yet, to this place are stationed the regular cooks, and besides all poultice, bits of toast, boiled eggs, warmed snacks, etc., must be cooked at that stove. Imagine the place then where the nurses, sisters and cooks were all intent, upon securing their portion of the mess. Black George, when about to remove from the oven large pans of cornbread or meat will swing his arms and their contents back and forth singing out, "Clar the way, Clar the way." Then each one must look out for herself to avoid a burning. Of course there is considerable ambition manifested on these occasions in order to secure the best "pot luck." A young black boy hopped up at a pot of mush saying to one of the sisters who was about to help herself, "Fust come, fust served." "Fust come you little rat, what do you mean?" said the sister, "Well" said the boy, "I'll go up and tell my sister and she's the crossest of the gang, and I say she'll have her share of the mush."

The house is now resuming quite an orderly appearance; the wards look clean, the patients improving. The sisters' rooms are in the second story, front building, but over the entrance their sitting room and dormitory is separated by the amputation room. After an amputation, the patient is usually brought out into the large room or passage opposite. There the sisters can attend at once to him, if needed. The dormitory looks very neat—little cots with blue spreads; the walls are of the red and white peculiar to unplastered bricks, but I guess people sleep right well there. Then the sitting room has the beginning of an altar in the shape of two wooden horses, with boards put across, a little table with a tin basin, drinking cup, etc., on it. Bags of old linen, bandages, things unmarked for the hospital, and a lot of chairs. Here we take our [spiritual] exercises as regularly as we can. After night prayers each sister picks up her chair and migrates to the dormitory. In the morning [she] brings the chair back again. The fare is substantial and good though we see but little milk or butter but the bread is excellent and very fresh. Old George's cornbread is hard to beat—if all goes on well no doubt, in a short time, it will be a splendid place.

There is a graveyard in front of the house and one at the side; it is convenient, at the same time it renders the house much more privacy than if it were on the open street. From the windows the view commands the City of Richmond, the surrounding country.[33] Now we expect your enthusiasm will be greatly roused, and after this account many will volunteer for *St. Ann's Military Hospital* [in the capital of the Confederacy].[34]

HARPERS FERRY

Military Hospital of Bolivar Heights. June 7, 1861, a telegram from Harpers Ferry, a town in [West] Virginia, on the border line, of the Potomac River, reached our peaceful home, St. Joseph's, asking for sisters to serve the sick soldiers of the Confederate Army.[35] Nearly every sister that could be spared was already engaged in the various locations where War's ravages had begun, but our zealous Superiors did their best here also, by sending them three sisters.[36]

On the 9th we left by stage for Frederick City, with a good outfit of prudence, caution, etc., from our dear Mother Ann Simeon [Norris], lest we meet trouble as we had the Northern Army and sentinels to pass. An escort had been sent for us, but the telegram had left him far behind, and we met our intended guide without knowing it, he passing on to St. Joseph's [Emmitsburg] for us. Our Lord, it seemed, wished the work to be His own.

An unexpected engagement kept villagers and farmers quietly at home, and men cautiously whispered their fears or opinions. To see people bold enough to travel just then was looked at with surprise. For this reason the sisters tried to sit back in the stage, hoping to pass unobserved, but, halting in a little town for mail, the driver, opening the stage door and handing a letter, said in a loud voice, "A gentleman in Emmitsburg desires you to put this letter in the Southern post office after you cross the line.

All eyes of the astonished people were on us, and we, too, were surprised, as we were not even aware of the driver's knowing our destination. However, nothing more was said and we passed on. The heat was excessive; one of our horses gave out. After some delay, we arrived in Frederick City. A few sentinels stood here and there, but no one noticed us, as the sisters were so often on the road. However, the knowing men of the city gathered round our carriage, saying, "Why, Ladies, where are you going?" Several asking questions at a time, we replied to those more easily answered, without their being better informed.

As hostilities had stopped the cars, we had to continue in a stage. A Southern lady and gentleman joined us here, who were trying to return South. Almost sick with the heat, we journeyed on until another horse gave out; here, again, suspense! The rocks of the Maryland heights on our right and the Potomac River on our left—here our carriage became fastened [stuck] in the road and we feared we should have to walk [the rest of] our way.

At last we proceeded and about twilight we saw the Southern pickets, for the South held a portion of Maryland still. The first picket inquired where we were going and to what intent. He then passed us on to the next and so on until we came to the last who said, "We have just received such strict orders as to crossing in or out, that it is not in my power to pass you on," but he sent for the Captain of the Guards and we were soon over the Potomac Bridge, on which kegs of gun powder were already placed so that the moment of the enemy's approach, it might be destroyed.

We alighted at the Military Hotel. The whole town [Harpers Ferry], nearly, was a barrack, and soldiers and Negroes were by far the majority of human beings to be seen.

The officer who received us said, "Sisters, you are not here too soon." He took us in, saying, our apartments would be ready for us directly, but the good pastor of the place, Reverend Doctor Costello, came immediately, telling the officer that there were more private arrangements made for us near the hospital and that he was ready to show them to us.[37] We followed the good priest on foot, the stage having gone away, not daring to stay on an enemy's shore. Every step for half a mile was an ascent, and never had a cornette been seen there.

Harpers Ferry, the town, is at the junction of the Potomac and Shenandoah Rivers, the Potomac separating Maryland and Virginia, while the Shenandoah runs into Central Virginia. Very high mountains bounded both rivers. Another height many, many feet above the town and between the two rivers was the Bolivar Height, on which our hospital stood.

The neat little Church was about midway between the valley or town, and the mount of our hospital. The hospital was filled with sick, and around the town lay about 40 or 50 thousand men just arrived from the most remote southern states, and a cold, wet spell having preceded the present heat, they were sick and lay in their tents until there were vacancies or turns for them in the better sheltered houses in the town. One regiment had contracted measles on its march, and this spreading among others in such exposure, thinned their numbers before the balls and swords had begun their quicker work.

On reaching our lodgings, supper was prepared, and soon we retired to bed. The stillness and darkness of the town were frightful. No sound but our own voices or footsteps was to be heard. Not a light gleamed from the thousand windows all over the place, for fear of a discovery to the hidden enemy. The whole army there had been sleeping or rather resting on their arms since their arrival, expecting hourly attack.

The Medical Director, he, who with the officer in charge of that section, had sent for us, came early in the morning to take us to the hospital. He, with his assistant, took us from room to room, introducing us to the sick, saying to them, "Now you will have no cause to complain of not getting medicine, drinks and nourishment in right time, for the Daughters of Charity will see to these things."

An apartment was given to us in the hospital. We noticed one man who seemed to be very low. He told us, on being asked, that he had never been baptized and hearing of its necessity, advantages, etc., he asked earnestly to receive it. We sent for the good Doctor Costello, who not only baptized him but formally christened him also. The poor man was fervent and grateful; looking at sister, who had spoken of it to him, he said to her, "May God bless you!" He died during the night. This was our first day of the Hospital.

This town had been by turns in the possession of North and South, and therefore completely drained of provisions, necessary conveniences for the sick, etc., so that the poor sick and all around them had much to suffer. Notwithstanding these difficult things were beginning to look more comfortable, when suddenly a telegram from Winchester, [Virginia], a town more central and much larger, came, ordering the whole Army with its accompaniments to repair there [Winchester] immediately.

WINCHESTER

Departure from Harpers Ferry. The North Army, it was rumored, was to cross the Potomac above and below us at some distance, and thus surrounding us, cut off all supplies whatever.[38] The Army moved at once, but they who served the sick, and those that were to collect tents, finally destroy bridges, rail tracks, etc., were still delayed some. Provisions were cast into the river to deprive the enemy of them. Then came new orders to wait awhile; but the poor sick had already been moved to the depot to wait there for the return of the cars from Winchester.

Before leaving the sick [in Harpers Ferry] for their removal, we instructed some who seemed not ill enough for baptism, that if they grew worse they must ask for that Sacrament, and in case of impossibility, they must offer their desires to Almighty God, etc. Two of these died, we heard, on their way to Winchester.

Arrangements were now being made for the several explosions and we were sent to remain with a worthy Catholic family, further from these buildings. During the night, one after another, the Grand Bridge in its turn shook heights, valley, and town. The little Church (Catholic), the only one that had not been applied to military purposes, was filled and surrounded by the frightened people. The poor worn-out Pastor, their only Consoler, and his weary breast the only safe spot for his gracious Lord to rest on.[39] He was nearly exhausted from former labors, attending the sick, hungry, sleepless, and constantly on foot. We looked at the awful destruction around us, and felt ourselves encompassed with desolation. All next day we expected hourly to be called to the cars, but no such word came.

We now heard that the Ladies of Winchester had written to the Medical Director, "not to have the Daughters of Charity serve the sick that they would wait on them." We knew also that those ladies had been enthusiastic in their favor in the comforts they from time to time had sent them.

Thinking, then, that our delay here was owing to the embarrassment the doctors might be in regarding this, we said to them: "Gentlemen, we are aware of the ardor with which the Winchester Ladies have labored for your poor men, as also of their desire to serve them alone, that is, without aid of ours. Therefore, be candid enough to allow us to return to our home, in case you feel any difficulty respecting the Ladies of Winchester. It is reasonable that they should wish to serve them themselves. We will not be pained, but rather truly grateful for your friendly candor, etc." They said, "No, they cared nothing for the objections that had been made to them on that matter; that those Ladies could never do for the sick as the Daughters of Charity would do, and therefore, unless we insisted on returning home, they held us to our undertaking." They begged us not to leave the town, but wait for the signal for departure. Expecting all day and even until 11:00 p.m. to be sent for, and

The Union Army departs from Harpers Ferry. Illustration by Wayne R. Warnock.

feeling rest absolutely necessary, we were getting into bed when the kind Lady of the house came into our room saying, ""my poor, dear sisters, the wagon and your baggage are at the door for you." We soon left our benevolent host who wept to see us pursuing hardships. An open farm wagon with two Negro men to drive, our worthy Pastor who was determined not to leave us entirely to strangers, and our good Lord, still on his breast, was to be our Blessed Guide and Companion. Our trunks formed seats for us. The heavy spray from both rivers was thick in the air; here and there a star appeared between broken clouds, giving barely light enough to see the Sentinel at his post, who in turn advanced, asking the countersign, that the good Pastor gave him. Our wagon running on a high terrace edge on the Potomac River made with the darkness, a gloomy prospect before us. On reaching the Depot, an officer met us, offered to find us a shelter until the car would arrive. He conducted us over two boards raised up, and by his lantern we could see water on one side of us, so that we must watch to pick our steps lest we might get off the boards. At last he opened a little hut, whose door was almost washed by the river; here we entered, sat down resting our foreheads on our umbrellas, until between 3 or 4 o'clock [in the morning], when taking the cars we arrived in Winchester in five hours.

Arrival in Winchester. Nearly the entire town was occupied by the soldiers, so that hotels were scarcely to be made use of. The one we went to seemed filled with the families, wives or sisters of the wealthier officers of the Southern Army, who came to be near them, for a vast Army now lay around the town. These Ladies, also those of the Hotel, received us even with affection, but had no room for us, save to rest an hour or two on the bed of the Lady of the house. After the poor priest had rested also, he said he would take us first to the Church, and then go in search of lodging for us. The Church, the poorest, poorest old stone building, stood in the suburbs. A crowd of ignorant men and women followed us as we walked. Taking the Blessed [Eucharistic] Host from his breast, the poor priest placed it on the altar; no Tabernacle there; then placing an altar card before it, he lit a candle.[40] The group that followed us crowded in and about the door, and when they saw us go by turn to the Confessional, they went around outside and peeped through the cracks at us, right in front of our face. While making our thanksgiving, the good Father went out, shutting the door hard after him, to get away [from] those people, we thought. Well, after we were tired [of] expecting him, we went to the door and really perceived we were prisoners, for the door was locked. We returned to prayer for the Gracious Companion of our journey was with us. After some time he returned, but truly we did fear the dear priest had lost his mind, and would not return. We knew his hardships had been excessive, besides being sick, without sleep or food. But he returned and took us to a plain, worthy Catholic family. Never had a Daughter of Saint Vincent been on that ground before.

The next morning being Sunday, we walked to Church. Just at the gate we had to halt to let a Company of Soldiers enter, we making the rear. About twenty or thirty Catholics made up the congregation, but on this day the Soldiers and sisters made quite an assembly. They had a band of Sunday School children, of about twelve in number; these their teachers brought to see us in the evening. We distributed medals, pictures, chaplets, etc., among them, making them very happy, as all those little matters were almost new to them.

We were waiting patiently for the Doctors to take us to our duty, as Reverend Doctor Costello had called on them from time to time, telling them we were anxious to be among the sick. They came for us after a few days, for the rest was really necessary for us, if rest it was, for here and there, the sisters were asked to go to such and such a house, to see some poor sick person. They were taken to see a Lutheran woman, whose husband was a Catholic. She was ill, doubted of her eternal safety because she believed more in the Catholic religion, but having sworn never to leave her own she could not, as she thought, hope for salvation if she broke her vow. She took the medal of our Immaculate Mother, however, from the sister and a visit or two finished the work of Divine grace in her soul, and she died with every desirable sentiment.

The Medical Director asked us if we must remain in one hospital, or would each sister take charge of a separate one? We told him our number was too small to divide, we would remain at this one; this was his own—heads of families remained in town, while grown up daughters and children were sent to Country Seats, the mothers of these staying at their houses in town and receiving and serving as many sick soldiers as they could. We received much kindness from these ladies, for they knew the common rations of the soldiers were, through quantity and quality, very, very wretched. Indeed our greatest distress as to the duty was, that we had not for the poor men what their suffering condition called for.

The Medical Director told us one day that he had gone to different families, and speaking of the Daughters of Charity in their hospital, all expressed their approbation and satisfaction, but one old maid (a prayer meeting devotee) who expressed her objection. The Doctor was very happy to tell us this. At one time we heard loud threats and angry jargon in our kitchen. Two sisters hastened there and found two colored men, a cook and a nurse fighting. The sisters forced them apart by stepping between them, and mildly requesting each man to calm himself. This was soon done.

Our house, every spot, was filled with sick and there was occasionally a death, but not very frequent, for as yet we had no wounded men. No Catholics, or very few were here, as that part of the South know but little of our holy religion, but nearly everyone that died in their senses accepted the spiritual assistance offered to them.

The labors began to show on our poor sisters, being but three in number, when the Doctor said there would be no way of sending for more, but by one of us to go home, since only the Daughters of Charity could travel now. She went partly by car, then stage, and a dangerous crossing the Potomac in a flat canoe, then on foot as fast as she could walk, and often running for a mile to reach the next car before it would leave, and here the cornette gained admission for her.[41] The evening of the next day she reached St. Joseph's [Emmitsburg], where she was received as if from the grave, for our anxious Superiors had heard nothing from or of us, except as public news told of the movements of the two armies. Our dear Sister Euphemia [Blenkinsop], now our Mother [for missions in the Confederacy], then left with three companions for Winchester, to relieve the sisters there. At the same time they telegraphed to dear Sister Valentine [Latouraudais], at St. Louis, to come immediately and replace our dear Sister Euphemia [Blenkinsop] in Winchester, as she was destined to proceed more southward, for in Richmond, Virginia, our sisters were almost overcome with duty, the severest battles having been fought in that section.[42]

Our dear sisters, now six in number, continued their labor in Winchester until very few remained in the hospitals, happy in seeing our holy religion casting sacred influence among the people, who until now, only knew how to condemn and despise it. The healthy and convalescing army had been leaving the place for some days towards Richmond. Our sisters there had been urging those in Winchester to come to their aid [in Richmond]; the sisters informed the doctors [at Winchester] that they wished to comply, as there were so few now to nurse. "Oh! No sisters," said the Doctor, "we cannot let you go while the hospital is open. See all our men well first." However, new appeals from Richmond brought new "petitions to be gone" by our sisters [to leave] here [Winchester], until the doctors consented, they having about ten or twelve sick then. Our kind friends there grieved to see the Cornettes leave their Town [or Winchester].

NORFOLK

Our Missions in Norfolk had for many years been in peaceful operation until 1861, the war between the North and the South, was beginning to be felt by us also.[43] April 28th brought its first violence, a bombardment of the two cities which were divided by a narrow neck of the sea or bay.

The establishments of the sisters were one hospital, St. Vincent's Hospital, an orphan asylum, and a day school.[44] The first thing to be done on hearing the terrible news was to place ourselves confidingly in the arms of Divine Providence; then placing a light before several statues of our Immaculate Mother, thus claiming her powerful assistance, we felt prepared for the issue.

Soon we beheld what the tolling bells had announced, the destructive fire! The Navy Yard of Portsmouth in flames! Large magazines of powder exploding shook the two cities to a fearful trembling. This occurred on Sunday morning. A heavy train of powder had been secretly laid, intending an entire overthrowing of the place but, an Infinite Power said here, as formerly: "Thus far, thou shalt go, but no farther," and they were spared.

The Confederate troops were filling Norfolk, and our hospital was crowded with sick. Many died, but baptisms and conversions were numerous. Those who recovered and left us have given evidence that a true idea of our holy religion had done its salutary work upon their souls.

PORTSMOUTH

Soon, however, Norfolk was evacuated. Norfolk and Portsmouth were taken by the North. As all that could leave before the coming of the Northern

The Navy Yard of Portsmouth in flames. Illustration by Wayne R. Warnock.

troops, had done so, our hospital was empty. The soldiers crowded into the city and great confusion followed for some days. Soon the Marine Hospital in Portsmouth was prepared for the sick and wounded, and the Northern Authorities asked for our sisters to attend them.

Portsmouth Marine Hospital

The necessity being urgent, the sister servants here sent as many as could be spared from their houses until Superiors could relieve them. Two days previous, hundreds of soldiers had arrived from the battlefield, in a deplorable condition. There was no time to be lost with regard to body or soul, for many we had cause to fear, had received mortal wounds in each. Some scarcely seemed to know God. Some were too low [frail] to understand their own misery.

Day and night our sisters constantly administered by turns to soul and body; nourishment, remedies and drinks to the body, and as best they could, "living waters to the soul." Indeed, as far as possible, our dear sisters subtracted from food and rest, the dying and suffering state of these poor men, causing them to make all sacrifices to them even joyfully, regarding such sacrifices as only a drop or cipher compared to the crying duties before them. While they were attending to some, others would be calling to them most piteously to give their wounds some relief.

Thanks to our dear Lord, many were baptized in apparently good dispositions.

In a few more days, several more sisters came to their aid from the Central House [Emmitsburg]. As if the enemy of souls wished to oppose their labors, they met with a delay on the road by being refused passports and again, barely escaped being lost in crossing a river in too small a boat for the number of passengers, but Divine Providence saved them.

With the assistance of this addition to their number, the sisters were enabled to effect more good, though Satan was always present as an obstacle in some way. Many Protestant army chaplains attended these wards and some of them zealously accompanied us from bed to bed, speaking in bland tones to the dying men: "How are you, my friend? Will you have the morning paper?" "The morning paper" to a dying man, and by a minister of the Gospel! A sister was applying cold applications to the head of a fever patient, when bursting into tears he exclaimed, "O, if my dear mother could see your care of me, she would take you to her heart."

A man of about twenty-three years of age saw a sister in a distance and, raising his voice he said, "Sister, come and pray awhile by my bed!" He was

Soldiers gathered around as the Sister prayed. Illustration by Wayne R. Warnock.

dying. Sister had just arrived at the hospital and felt as yet, untutored, but she knelt by his bed and made suitable aspirations for him in a low voice. With clasped hands he repeated all in a very loud tone, begged God to pardon him, then prayed to our Blessed Mother, his Angel Guardian and to all the angels to conduct him to Heaven.

Sister said, "I will go away if you pray so loud." "O, sister," he replied, "I want God to know that I am in earnest!" Sister showed him her crucifix, saying, "Do you know what this means?" He took it, kissed it reverently, and then said, "Jesus <u>hammered</u> on the cross for me! Jesus <u>whipped</u> to death for me! Will you not receive me?" Sister continued to assist him not knowing that anyone was near until presently the dying man, perceiving a companion said, "George, come here and hear what sister is telling me." She looked up and saw a wall of human beings around her, drawn by the loud prayers of the poor man. In this crowd and on his knees was one of the doctors, a Protestant, who being on his rounds among the patients, seeing sister on her knees praying, had involuntarily knelt and remained so until sister rose to prepare a table near the bed, as the priest had been sent for.

While sister was getting other things ready, the good doctor brought a table covered with a pillow case, two black bottles for candle sticks and common tallow candles already lighted, in them. The poor man kept crying out as loud as he could, "Sister, come. Sister, come."

As soon as the sister left him, a minister went to him and said, "My friend, I perceive you are dying. Let me assist you by prayer to go to heaven." The dying man interrupted him with: "Begone from me; I would never reach there by your hands." The poor preacher, who but a few days before was a carpenter, turned away disappointed.

The assembled crowd was present at the last anointing and reception of the Holy Viaticum. Some asked sister to show them Scripture for these sacraments. The doctor applied to the priest for information.

The sick man died, begging God to bless the sisters and calling on angels to present his soul to God.

This was followed by several other edifying deaths, for the faith resignation of such excited others to desire the same hopes of salvation.

A wretched man, who seemed to hate the sisters, refused his medicine and tried to strike them and spit upon them when they would offer it to him. After often acting in this manner, and finding that the sister still hoped he would take it, (for his life depended on it), he said, "Who or what are you anyway?"

Sister said, "I am a Sister of Charity." "Where is your husband?" he said. "I have none," said sister, "and I am glad I have none. "Why are you glad?" he asked, still very angry. "Because," she replied, "if I had a husband, I would have to be employed in his affairs, and consequently could not be here to wait on you." As if by magic in a subdued tone he said, "that will do," and turning his face from her, he remained silent.

Sister left him but returned presently and offered the medicine to him. He took it and motioned to her to sit down. Although he seemed near death, the medicine cured him and he was very soon a true friend of the Sisters, but so ignorant of religion in every way that he hardly knew he had a soul. Here again, our good Lord accepted our efforts to gain Him another soul, for the poor man with instruction, became as fervent as he had been indifferent.

A fine looking gentleman, dangerously wounded, was the object of the doctors' deepest interest and they begged the sister not to leave him alone. The sister spoke to him of God's infinite goodness, His tender Providence of the human family, etc. He listened attentively and seemed to enjoy the remarks she made. She withdrew and presently another sister approached him and inquired as to his condition, comfort, etc.

He said he felt better, and much consoled in an entertainment with a pious lady of his own persuasion, (much encouraged). "Where is she?"

said Sister, "There," said he, pointing to the one who had just left him, "and judging by your costume, I take you to be one also." Sister replied, "Yes, we are alike in creed." He raised his eyes to heaven saying, "Thank God, I am surrounded by my own true people!" "What!" said sister, "are you a Catholic?" Shocked through all his frame, he said "I! No, no! I am a Methodist." Later he seemed thoughtful; in the end he was baptized and died, we hoped, in good dispositions.

A young man in a dying state, said to sister, "Write to my mother and tell her that I was cared for in my sufferings by a band of ladies who were as tender to me as mothers." He asked for baptism and said soon after: "Where will I be tomorrow morning?" sister said, "I hope in heaven, with your Heavenly Father." "Oh!" he exclaimed, "in Heaven with God!" He entertained himself with God in most fervent acts and died in a consoling manner.

If we were to relate each one separately, the narratives would be too lengthy. It will do to say and to know that there were many baptisms and several conversions.

We had been at Portsmouth but about six months when the hospital was closed, and the authorities pointed out other locations. Several of our sisters were disposed in more pressing miseries and a few were bound for the Central House. The cars took them to Manassas, where an extensive encampment was, and in the midst of which they stopped. The sisters were told that they could not cross the Potomac as the enemy was firing on all who appeared. There was a little hut there and a Protestant family dwelling in it. It was there that the Army Chaplain celebrated Mass, one of the trunks serving for an altar.

They were obliged to go to Richmond, and it was two weeks before a flag of truce could take them to Maryland.

When all were on board, an officer visited the passengers in the cabin. Among them were several Southern ladies, and some of us had also been in the South for some time. When he saw us he exclaimed, "I need not question you, sisters; all is right with you. You mind your own business and don't meddle with government affairs. Your Society has done great service to the Country, and the Authorities in Washington hold your Community in high esteem."

This officer was the Judge Advocate and showed the sisters every kind attention. When the papers belonging to the passengers were asked for, we offered our letters. He said resentfully, "Let me see the man who would dare touch papers belonging to a Sister of Charity! I would give him cause to regret it." Then suddenly he said, "Give me your papers;" and taking them he wrote in large letters, "Examined." "Now," he continued, "take them; they are safe now."

While he was taking register of the names, some of the ladies looked out of humor; so on coming to the sisters he said, "O, here are faces I like to see! They are cheerful as if the peace of Heaven rested in their hearts, no gloom, and no frowns here."

When we reached Fortress Monroe, we wished to take the boat direct for Baltimore, but our kind friend said, "No." He did not often have the honor of having Daughters of Charity on his boat, and as we were rebels we were not over-stocked with money. On his boat we could travel free of expense, while on the other we would have to pay a high fare.

We reached Annapolis too late for the train to Baltimore, but our kind old friend chartered a train for our accommodation, and having paid our way through, bade us farewell. We felt his kindness the more as he knew that we had been nursing the Southern soldiers. To be sure, he may have seen us also at Portsmouth serving the North. At least he knew that "party" did not influence us in our labors for the poor men. We arrived home safely.[45]

MANASSAS

Manassas. Left Richmond for Manassas on the 9th of January 1862, at the solicitation of Doctor Williams, Medical Director of the Army of the Potomac.[46] We were five in number and found on taking possession, 500 patients, sick and wounded of both armies. Mortality was very great, as the poor sick had been very much neglected. The wards were in a most deplorable condition, and strongly resisted all efforts of the broom to which they had long been strangers, and the aid of a shovel was found necessary. At best, they were but poor protection against the inclemency of the season, and being scattered, we were often obliged to go through snow over a foot deep, to wait on the sick.

For our own accommodation we had one small room, which served for dormitory, Chapel, etc., which when we were fortunate enough to get a Chaplain, the Holy Sacrifice was daily offered in a little corner of our humble domicile. The kitchen, to which what we called our refectory was attached. I do not think I exaggerate when I say it was a quarter of a mile from our room. Often it was found more prudent to be satisfied with two meals, than to trudge through the snow for a third, which at best, was not very inviting, for the culinary department was not under our control, but under that of Negroes, who had a decided aversion for cleanliness.

On an average, ten died every day, and of this number, I think I may safely say, four were baptized, either by Fathers Smoulders or Teeling, or by our sisters. It happened several times that men, who had been until then totally ignorant of our faith, and I may say even of God, sent to us in the middle of the night, when they found that they were dying, and begged for baptism, which astonished as well as consoled and edified us.

On the 15th of March we received orders from General Johnson to pack up quietly and be ready to leave on six hours notice, as it was found necessary to retreat from that quarter. Oh, the horrors of War! We had scarcely left our post than the whole camp was one mass of flame, and the bodies of those who died that day were consumed.

GORDONSVILLE

Our next field of labor was the Military Hospital, Gordonsville. We were but three in number and found 200 patients very sick, pneumonia, and typhoid fever prevailing. Here again privations were not wanting. The sick were very poorly provided for, though the mortality was not as great as at Manassas. We had a small room which served again for <u>all</u> <u>purposes</u>. One week we lay on the floor without beds—our habits and a shawl loaned us by the doctor serving for covering. The refectory as far as distance is concerned, was more convenient, but accommodations were even less extravagant than at Manassas. The trunk of a tree was our table and the rusty tin cups and plates which were used in turn by doctors, sisters, and Negroes, were very far from exciting a great relish for what they contained.

Father Smoulders who was Chaplain at that time received about twenty-five into the Communion of the Church, some of whom died shortly after. One morning as Sister Estelle was visiting her patients before Mass, one called from the lower end of the ward, "Oh! Sister, sister do come and save me, let me die in the Church to which you sisters belong. I believe all that you believe."

Father Smoulders who was vesting for Mass, was at first unwilling to wait on him until after, but as sister insisted that no time was to be lost, he went and baptized him. As we knelt at the "Et Verbum Caro factum. est.," he expired.

DANVILLE

The approach of the Federals compelled us to leave Gordonsville on Easter Sunday, and we retreated "<u>in good order</u>" to Danville. Having been obliged to stop in Richmond sometime, we did not enter on the new field until the 2nd of May. Here we found 400 sick, much better provided for than in Manassas or Gordonsville. The sisters had a nice little house, which would have been a kind of luxury had it not been the abode of innumerable rats, of whom we stood in the greatest awe, for they seemed to be proprietors of the mansion. During the night shoes, stockings, etc., were carried off, and indeed, safe we did not feel for our fingers and toes which we often found, on waking, locked in the teeth of our bold visitors.

Most of our patients were Catholic, at least in name, for many had almost forgotten their duties as such, but it was our consolation to see them entering again upon them with the simplicity of children. The zeal of good Father Smoulders led many to a knowledge of our holy religion and about 50 were baptized.

LYNCHBURG

In November, the Medical Director removed our hospital to Lynchburg as there were no means of heating that in Danville. Our number [of Sisters] had increased to five as the hospital was larger and contained 1,000 patients, whom we found in a most pitiful condition.[47] The persons who were in charge, had a very good will, but not the means of carrying it out, and although the fund was ample, the poor patients were half starved, owing entirely to mismanagement.

As we passed through the ward the first time, accompanied by the doctor, a man from the lower end called out, "Lady, oh Lady, for God's sake give me a piece of bread." To give you an idea of the care the sick had received, it will be sufficient to say that, though the whole establishment had been cleaned for our reception some of the sisters swept up the vermin on the dust pan. The doctors soon placed everything under our control, and with a little economy, the patients were well provided for, and order began to prevail.

Father [Louis-Hippolyte] Gache, [S.J.,] a zealous and holy priest, affected much good and removed many prejudices from the minds of those whom a faulty education had made enemies—bitter enemies of our holy faith.[48] During the three years that we remained in Lynchburg, he baptized 100. Of those who resumed the practice of duties long neglected, we kept no account, but scarcely a day passed without witnessing the return of some poor prodigal.

During the year 1863, the Methodists and Baptists had a grand revival in Lynchburg, and every day members of both, ladies and gentlemen came to induce the officers and privates to attend, hoping to effect their conversion. Meeting one in whom they seemed to take a particular interest, I asked if their zeal and perseverance had not made at least some impression. He answered,

"No, that the modest silence of our sisters spoke far more loudly than the enthusiastics even of his own persuasion."

The approach of the Federals placed our hospital in imminent danger and it was decided to move the sick and the hospital stores to Richmond. Father [Hippolyte] Gache, accompanied us and continued his mission of zeal and charity.

ENDNOTES

1 Pope Paul VI canonized Saint Elizabeth Ann Seton September 14, 1975.

2 Through the nineteenth century the terms Sisters of Charity and Daughters of Charity were used interchangeably when referring to the Emmitsburg community. The correct title from 1809-1849 was Sisters of Charity of St. Joseph's (or simply Sisters of Charity) and from 1850 to the present, Daughters of Charity of Saint Vincent de Paul (or Daughters of Charity). There are other congregations of women religious in North America which trace their roots to the 1809 foundation at Emmitsburg and are also Sisters of Charity.

3 Rev. J. Francis Burlando, C.M., to Mother Gilbert-Elise Montcellet, D.C., January 7, 1862, included in "Notice on Our Sisters of the Province of the United States," *Lives of Our Deceased Sisters and Other Notices, 1854-1869* (Emmitsburg, MD: Daughters of Charity, 1869), 22. Hereinafter cited as *Lives and Notices, 1854-1869*.

4 6.93 Elizabeth Bayley Seton to Robert Goodloe Harper, December 28, 1811, Regina Bechtle, S.C., and Judith Metz, S.C., eds., Ellin M. Kelly, mss. ed., *Elizabeth Bayley Seton Collected Writings*, 3 vols. (New City Press: New York, 2000-2006), 2:206. Hereinafter cited as *CW*.

5 6.39 Elizabeth Bayley Seton to Antonio Filicchi, May 20, 1810, *CW* 2:127.

6 By this time, the Daughters of Charity had establishments in Philadelphia, New York, Baltimore, Frederick, Washington, Harrisburg, Albany, St. Louis, Cincinnati, Wilmington, New Orleans, Boston, Mobile, Detroit, Rochester, Milwaukee, Natchez, Buffalo, Syracuse, Santa Barbara, Norfolk, Richmond, and Chicago.

7 See Mary Denis Maher, C.S.A., *To Bind Up the Wounds. Catholic Sister Nurses in the U.S. Civil War* (Louisiana State University Press: Baton Rouge, 1989), 37.

8 The Daughters of Charity also served in the Spanish American War and in World War I.

9 Sister Matilda Coskery, D.C., "Frederick," *Notes of the Sisters Services in Military Hospitals, 1861-1865*, 140. Hereinafter cited as Notes.

10 Rev. J. Francis Burlando, C.M., to Mother Gilbert-Elise Montcellet, D.C., September 1, 1862, included in "Notice on Our Sisters of the Province of the United States," *Lives and Notices, 1854-1869*, 29.

11 Although records list 232 names of sisters missioned to wartime nursing by Emmitsburg, local sister servants had delegated authority to send sisters to meet emergency needs in their region. This accounts for the involvement of over 300 sisters in total. Daniel Hannefin, D.C., *Daughters of the Church* (New City Press: New York, 1987), 110. See also Sister Angela Tully, D.C., *Maryland in the Civil War* (Unpublished thesis. Canisius College, Buffalo, NY, 1933), ASJPH, 51.

12 Mother Margaret O'Keefe, D.C., to Helen Ryan Jolly, [n.d.] 1918, quoted in Helen Ryan Jolly, *Nuns of the Battlefield*, (Providence, RI: Visitor Press, 1927), 59.

[13] Father Burlando, was director of the Daughters of Charity for twenty years (1853-1873). He along with Mother Ann Simeon Norris (1816-1866), orchestrated the corporate response of the community during the Civil War and it aftermath. Burlando requested that the sisters submit memoranda of their experiences of wartime nursing.

[14] Rev. J. Francis Burlando, C.M., to the Daughters of Charity of the Province of the United States, October 30, 1866, Notes.

[15] Ibid.

[16] *Daughters of Charity Annals of the Civil War.*

RICHMOND

[17] *St. Francis de Sales Infirmary* may also have been known as the Catholic Charitable Hospital. Sister Rose Noyland, Sister Juliana Chatard, and Sister Anna Louise O'Connell contributed to this account. See also Rebecca Barbour Calcutt, *Richmond's Wartime Hospitals* (Gretna, Louisiana: Pelican Publishing Company, 2005).

[18] The sisters did not arrive on this date.

[19] The sister servants at this time of the Richmond missions were Sister Juliana Chatard at *St. Francis de Sales Infirmary*, and Sister Rose Noyland at *St. Joseph's Asylum*.

[20] It was customary in community that a small bell was rung to summon the sisters to their spiritual exercises.

[21] The Seven Days Battle, June 25-July 1, 1862.

[22] The bracket portion of text was omitted from the 1904 edition of this document but appears in the source document.

[23] This date is when Dr. Gibson asked for the Daughters of Charity. July 26th is also the liturgical feast of Saint Ann, mother of Mary of Nazareth, for whom the sisters named *St. Ann's Military Hospital.*

[24] There were a series of twenty-eight temporary hospitals referred to by numeric designation as the General Hospital (#1-#28). This refers to General Hospital #1 (aka the *Alms House Hospital* or *St. Ann's Military Hospital*) located opposite Shockoe Cemetery on the north side of Hospital Street, between 2nd and 4th Streets.

[25] John McGill was bishop of the diocese of Richmond, 1850-1872.

[26] Cf. Judith 13.

[27] This refers to the *Alms House Hospital* (aka General Hospital #1 or *St. Ann's Military Hospital*).

[28] These sisters stayed initially with the Daughters of Charity at *St. Joseph's Asylum*, 4th and Marshall Streets.

[29] Sister Blanche Rooney went to Richmond July 26, 1861. There is no record of a Daughter of Charity by the name of Sister Blanche DeLaney.

[30] A written note with one such pen and ink sketch provides details about the signed artwork.

[31] Holy Water has received a special blessing and is considered a sacramental.

[32] Refers to the descendants of Elizabeth Bayley Seton (1774-1821) and William Magee Seton (1768-1803) and to Major General Robert Goodloe Harper (1765-1825), who married Catherine Carroll, a daughter of Charles Carroll of Carrollton, who was cousin to Archbishop John Carroll. The Harpers were friends of the Daughters of Charity at Emmitsburg. Henry and William Seton, grandsons of Saint Elizabeth Ann Seton, served in the United States Army during the Civil War. Captain Henry Seton, 54th New York Regiment, served under General Eliamkim P. Scammon and Gen. John G. Foster. Captain William Seton, 4th Regiment, United States Volunteers, and was twice severely wounded in the battle of Antietam. After recovering he was Captain, 16th Artillery during General Ulysses S. Grant's campaign against Richmond.

[33] This may be the same person who is identified as General Ricketts in the 1861 pen and ink sketch by a Union prisoner.

[34] Located on the northwestern edge of Richmond, on a hill, the adjacent cemetery was a popular spot from which to view the smoke and exploding shells of distant battlefields on Church Hill, Chimborazo Hospital (1862-1865), provided a similar venue and was a complex of hospital wards, with five divisions, often referred to as Chimborazo Hospital #1, #2, #3, #4, and #5.

HARPERS FERRY

[35] Sister Matilda Coskery wrote this account of the Daughters of Charity at Harpers Ferry.

[36] The following Daughters of Charity were the first to serve at Harpers Ferry: Sister Matilda Coskery, Sister Frances Karrer, and Sister Lucina Maher.

[37] The title "Reverend Doctor" indicates a clergyman with some advanced education or degree.

WINCHESTER

[38] Sister Matilda Coskery wrote this account of the departure of the Daughters of Charity from Harpers Ferry and their time in Winchester.

[39] Refers to Eucharistic altar bread used for communion in the celebration of the Sacred Liturgy.

[40] The prayers of the Mass were printed on altar cards for the convenience of the celebrant of the Sacred Liturgy.

[41] Probably Sister Matilda Coskery.

[42] Sister Euphemia Blenkinsop was the official representative of the superiors of the Daughters of Charity at Emmitsburg for the sisters on missions throughout the Confederacy since November 1861.

NORFOLK AND PORTSMOUTH

[43] The Daughters of Charity had opened *St. Vincent's Hospital* (1857) and *St. Mary's Asylum* (1848) in Norfolk.

[44] A select school for day pupils had been operated by the sisters at *St. Mary's Orphan Asylum* since 1848.

[45] Sister Mary Angela Heath and Sister Anna Louise O'Connell wrote accounts of the sisters services in Portsmouth and Norfolk during the Civil War.

MANASSAS, GORDONSVILLE, DANVILLE, AND LYNCHBURG

[46] Sister Mary Angela Heath wrote accounts of the Daughters of Charity at Manassas, Gordonsville, Danville, Lynchburg, and Richmond.

[47] The Daughters of Charity worked in the hospital at Ferguson's Tobacco Factory. The sisters also spent time assisting in the Pest House under the direction of John J. Terrell, M.D., in 1862. The sisters, who were sent from Richmond remained in Lynchburg to nurse the wounded until 1865.

[48] See Louis-Hippolyte Gache, *A Frenchman, A Chaplain, A Rebel: The War Letters of Rev. Louis-Hippolyte Gache*, trans., Cornelius M. Buckley (Chicago: Loyola University Press, 1981).